Numbers and You

Robyn O'Sullivan

Contents

Introduction

If you were asked to use numbers to tell about your body, what would you say? You might say you have two eyes. You might say you have ten fingers. These are just two ways you could use numbers to tell about your body. Let's find other numbers that can tell about you!

206 Bones

Did you know that babies have more bones in their bodies than adults? Newborn babies have 300 bones in their bodies, but adults only have 206. How can that be? As babies grow, some of their bones join together. That's why adults have fewer bones.

Imagine your body without bones. You wouldn't be able to stand up! That's because your bones form a frame called a **skeleton**. Your skeleton gives your body shape.

All the bones in your body fit together to form a skeleton.

As babies grow, some of their bones join together.

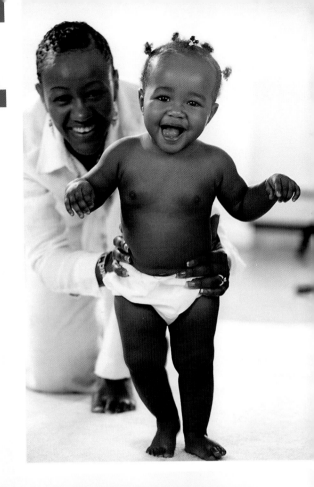

figure It Out

How many more bones does a baby have than an adult?

Number of bones in a baby	300
Number of bones in an adult	− 206
	94

A baby has **94** more bones than an adult.

Some bones protect parts of your body. Run your fingers along the sides of your belly. Can you feel your ribs? Your ribs are like a cage of bones in your chest. They protect your heart and lungs.

Other bones work with muscles so you can move. The bones in your feet and legs help you to stand up and walk. The bones in your hands and fingers help you to pick things up.

We use the bones in our hands when we tie our shoelaces.

An X-ray shows the 27 bones in a hand.

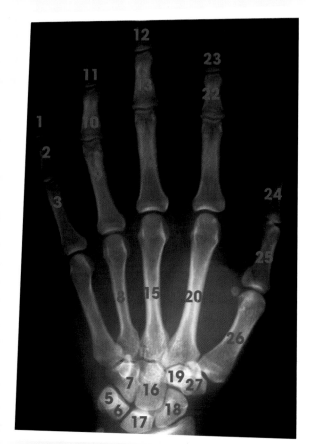

Figure It Out

There are 27 bones in a human hand. How many bones are in two hands?

Number of bones in one hand	27
Number of bones in the other hand	+ 27
	54

There are **54** bones in two hands.

32 Teeth

What would you do without teeth? You use your teeth to bite and chew food. Teeth also help you to talk clearly. They help shape many of the sounds in your mouth when you talk.

Most adults have 32 teeth. However, they don't have 32 teeth their entire lives. Babies are born with 20 teeth inside their gums. The teeth start to push through the gums when a baby is about six months old. When a child is about six years old, these baby teeth start to fall out. Adult teeth grow back in their place.

Teeth help us to break food into bite-size pieces.

Most people lose their front teeth when they are six or seven years old.

figure It Out

How many more teeth do adults grow than children?

Number of teeth in an adult	32
Number of teeth in a child	− 20
	12

Adults grow **12** more teeth than children.

660 Muscles

There are about 660 muscles in the human body. Different kinds of muscles do different things. The muscles in your arms and legs help you to walk and pick up things. You can control these muscles.

Other muscles work by themselves. Your heart is a muscle that helps to pump blood throughout your body. This happens without you thinking about it.

We use our muscles in gym class.

We use more muscles when we frown than when we smile.

figure It Out

People use 40 muscles when they frown, but only 20 muscles when they smile. How many more muscles does it take to frown than to smile?

Number of muscles in a frown	40
Number of muscles in a smile	− 20
	20

It takes **20** more muscles to frown than to smile.

100,000 Hairs

How many hairs do you have on your head? Are there more than 1,000? Yes. More than 10,000? Yes! Most people have about 100,000 hairs on their head. Hair keeps your head warm. It also helps to protect the skin on your head from the sun.

It would take a long time to count every single hair on your head.

Hair grows about half an inch every month. Hair grows out of **follicles**. These are small tubes in the skin. When a hair finishes growing, it falls out. Then a new hair grows from the follicle.

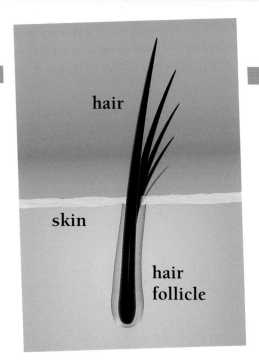

hair

skin

hair follicle

Each hair grows out of a hair follicle beneath the skin.

Figure It Out

If hair grows 6 inches in one year, how many inches will it grow in two years?

Number of inches hair grows in year one	6
Number of inches hair grows in year two	+ 6
	12

Hair grows about **12** inches in two years.

1,800 Breaths

When we breathe, we take in **oxygen** from the air. People need oxygen to make their bodies work. Children breathe about 30 times a minute when resting, or sitting still. That means they take about 1,800 breaths in an hour!

When you exercise, you breathe faster. When you run or swim, you might breathe 60 times in a minute. You breathe faster because your body needs more oxygen.

We can use our breath to blow bubbles.

We breathe faster when we are active.

figure It Out

About how many breaths do children take in an hour? Use a calculator to **multiply** and find out.

Number of breaths taken in a minute	30
Number of minutes in an hour	× 60
	1,800

Children breathe about **1,800** times in an hour.

100,800 Heartbeats

Why does your heart beat?
Your heart beats to pump blood
around your body. It beats
about 70 times a minute.
That's about 4,200 times
an hour, and 100,800 times
a day! The blood travels in tubes
called **blood vessels**.

You can't see the blood in your
body. But you can feel your
heart beating in your chest.
You can also feel blood
pumping through some of
your blood vessels. This is
called your **pulse**. The easiest
places to feel your pulse are
on your neck or your wrist.

You can use two fingers
to take your pulse.

A doctor uses a special tool to hear your heart beat.

figure It Out

How many times does a person's heart beat in a day? Use a calculator to **multiply** and find out.

Number of heartbeats in an hour	4,200
Number of hours in a day	x 24
	100,800

Your heart beats about **100,800** times in a day.

1,500 Blinks

Most people blink about 25 times every minute. That's about 1,500 times every hour! Every time you blink, tears come out of your upper eyelids. The eyelids spread the tears across your eyes as you blink. The tears wash away **germs** and dirt in your eyes. The tears also keep your eyes from drying out.

Your eyes don't stay open all the time. They would dry out if they did.

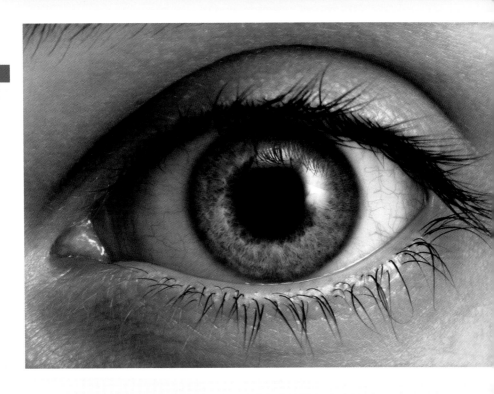

Most people blink about once every two seconds.

figure It Out

How many times does a person blink in an hour?
Use a calculator to **multiply** and find out.

Number of blinks in a minute	25
Number of minutes in an hour	x 60
	1,500

You blink about **1,500** times each hour.

Measuring Up

Numbers can tell you a lot about your body. Can you think of two parts of your body that might be the same length? Use a measuring tape to find out.

Measure your forearm from the inside of your elbow to the end of your wrist.

First, measure the length of your forearm from the inside of your elbow to your wrist. Then, measure the length of your foot. Is your foot shorter, longer, or the same as your forearm?

Measure your foot from the back of your heel to the tip of your big toe.

Besides measuring your body, you can also measure many things your body can do. How far can you jump? How high can you stretch? What else can you count or measure about the human body?

Glossary

blood vessel   a tube that carries blood inside your body

follicle   a small tube under the skin out of which a hair can grow

germ   a tiny living thing that can cause disease

oxygen   a gas that is part of the air we breathe

pulse   the pumping of blood through your blood vessels

skeleton   all the bones of a body connected together

Index